BUILDING BLOCKS OF MATTER

CHEMICAL REACTIONS

Louise and Richard Spilsbury

Heinemann Library
Chicago, Illinois

© 2007 Heinemann Library
a division of Reed Elsevier Inc.
Chicago, Illinois

Customer Service 888-454-2279
Visit our website at www.heinemannraintree.com

Designed by Richard Parker and Tinstar Design Ltd, www.tinstar.co.uk
Printed and bound in China by Leo Paper Group

11 10 09 08 07
10 9 8 7 6 5 4 3 2 1

Library of Congress Cataloging-in-Publication Data
Spilsbury, Louise.
  Chemical reactions / Louise and Richard Spilsbury.
     p. cm. -- (Building blocks of matter)
  Includes bibliographical references and index.
  ISBN-13: 978-1-4034-9337-8 (lib. bdg.)
  ISBN-10: 1-4034-9337-5 (lib. bdg.)
  ISBN-13: 978-1-4034-9342-2 (pbk.)
  ISBN-10: 1-4034-9342-1 (pbk.)
  1. Chemistry--Juvenile literature. 2. Chemical reaction, Conditions and
laws of--Juvenile literature. I. Spilsbury, Richard, 1963- II. Title.
  QD35.S66 2007
  541'.39--dc22
                          2006025745

Acknowledgments
The publishers would like to thank the following for permission to reproduce photographs: Alamy p. **13** (Phil Degginger); Corbis pp. **20** (Paul A. Souders), **8** (Post-Houserstock/Dave G. Houser), **12** (Yogi, Inc.), **25** (Yves Forestier), **11**; Corbis/Bettmann p. **18**; Getty Images pp. **4** (National Geographic/Skip Brown), **17** (Photographer's Choice/Jeff Hunter); Harcourt Education Ltd./Tudor Photography pp. **11** top & bottom, **15**, **21**, **23** top & bottom; Masterfile pp. **19** (Gary Rhijnsburger), **24** (Kathleen Finlay), **16** (Mark Tomalty); Photolibrary.com pp. **27** (Frances Andrijich), **14** (Index Stock/Yvette Cardozo), **26** (Neil Duncan), **5** (Photononstop), **7** (Phototake Inc.); Science Photo Library p. **10** left & right (Andrew Lambert Photography).

Cover photograph of rusty metal reproduced with permission of Alamy/Imagestate.

Every effort has been made to contact copyright holders of any material reproduced in this book. Any omissions will be rectified in subsequent printings if notice is given to the publishers.

The publishers would like to thank Nick Sample for his help with the preparation of this book.

Disclaimer
All the Internet addresses (URLs) given in this book were valid at the time of going to press. However, due to the dynamic nature of the Internet, some addresses may have changed, or sites may have changed or ceased to exist since publication. While the author and publishers regret any inconvenience this may cause readers, no responsibility for any such changes can be accepted by either the author or the publishers.

Contents

Any words appearing in the text in bold, **like this**, are explained in the Glossary.

What Are Chemical Reactions?

Every substance has **physical properties**. For example, marbles are hard, round, and colorful. Flour is a soft white or brown powder. Physical properties describe what a substance looks and feels like. They are a way for us to compare things. If you mixed a handful of marbles and a handful of flour in a bowl, they would get mixed up. However, their physical properties would not change.

Some materials undergo a change when mixed together. They become a different material. This type of change is called a **chemical reaction**. When we mix concrete to make buildings or roads, a chemical reaction takes place. Soft cement powder and water mix together to make hard concrete. Concrete has different physical properties than both water and cement.

In this herd of wild animals, zebra and wildebeest mix together. But the physical properties of these animals are different from one another.

Chemical properties and change

A **chemical property** describes how well a material combines with others. For example, wood can combine with oxygen and burn. However, water cannot. They have different chemical properties. When wood burns, it turns into ash. Its physical and chemical properties change. Wood is brown and hard, but the ash is powdery and black. The ash cannot burn.

You can also change a substance without changing its chemical properties. Chopping wood into little pieces makes it look different. However, this is only a **physical change**. Each small piece of wood still has the same chemical properties as a large piece.

No going back

You could use a sieve to separate the flour and marble mixture. The change from separate materials to mixture is **reversible**. Chemical reactions are usually **irreversible**. Once they have happened, the new material cannot be turned back into the original materials.

Cooking uses irreversible chemical reactions. Once you have made a pancake, you cannot change it back into eggs, flour, and water.

5

How Do Chemical Reactions Work?

Everything in the world, from people to mountains to computers, is made from **matter**. **Atoms** are the smallest units of matter. There are about 115 different types of atom. **Chemical reactions** occur when different atoms combine and join together.

Changing atoms

Every atom has a central section called a **nucleus**. Very tiny **particles** called **electrons** whizz around the nucleus. Different atoms have different numbers of electrons. The electrons do not usually travel far from the nucleus because there is a force pulling them toward it. This force is similar to **magnetism**.

During a chemical reaction, electrons move. Sometimes the nucleus of one atom pulls an electron away from another atom. Other times, two atoms share an electron. When this happens, the two atoms join or **bond** together. Two or more atoms joined together form a **molecule**.

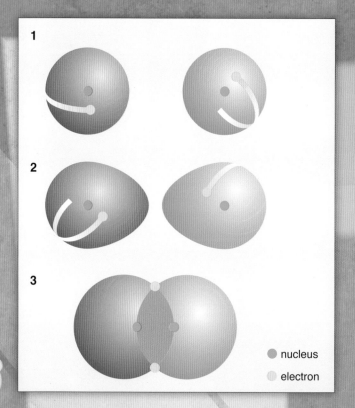

When two atoms approach (1), their electrons sometimes move (2) and are shared by both, forming a molecule (3).

● nucleus
● electron

Energy

Atoms need energy to **react**. The energy helps them get close enough to other atoms or molecules for electrons to move. Atoms and molecules are always **vibrating**. Heat is a form of energy. It makes atoms vibrate more than usual. Reactions often happen faster when substances get warmer. This is because they have more energy to collide with each other and to share or exchange electrons.

Reactivity

Matter that is made up of just one type of atom is called an **element**. When elements join together to form a new substance, it is called a **compound**. Some elements combine to form compounds more easily than others. For example, hydrogen reacts easily with many other elements, but neon does not. We say that hydrogen is more reactive than neon. The **reactivity** of any element depends on how tightly it holds onto its electrons.

Sodium **metal** is very reactive. It is normally kept under oil to stop it from reacting with oxygen in the air.

Did you know?
Precious metal

Gold is a metal that it is very **unreactive**. Gold atoms do not react with atoms in air or water. This means that gold always looks shiny and attractive. More reactive metals, such as copper, react with other atoms to form compounds on their surface. This makes the metal look duller or even makes it change color.

Elements together

Scientists arrange the elements in a special chart called the **periodic table**. The elements are grouped according to their reactivity and other properties. The position of each element in the table helps scientists to predict how it will react with other types of atom.

Gold is good for making jewelry because it is unreactive. It will stay shiny.

Writing reactions

Every element has its own **chemical symbol**. This is a letter or group of letters that acts as a short name. For example, carbon is C and gold is Au. We use chemical symbols to write down what happens during a chemical reaction. The symbols show how the atoms combine to form a new substance. Numbers are used to show how many atoms of each kind are in a molecule. For example, a molecule of H_2O (water) has two hydrogen atoms and one oxygen atom.

When writing a chemical reaction, the left-hand side shows the substances that react. These are called the **reactants**. The right-hand side shows the new substance formed during the reaction. It is called the **product**.

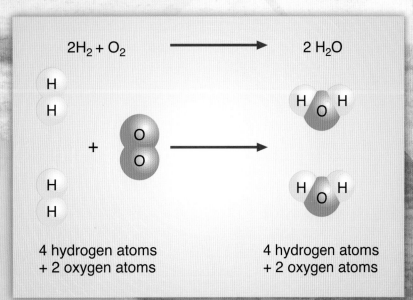

$$2H_2 + O_2 \longrightarrow 2\,H_2O$$

4 hydrogen atoms + 2 oxygen atoms

4 hydrogen atoms + 2 oxygen atoms

Four hydrogen atoms and two oxygen atoms combine to make two molecules of H_2O (water).

Adding up

Atoms are not destroyed during chemical reactions. The reactants' atoms still exist, but they are now part of the product. For example, oxygen and hydrogen atoms become part of water molecules. The number of atoms in the reactants is always the same as the number of atoms in the product. The **mass** of the substances also does not change.

What Changes Happen During Reactions?

A **chemical reaction** causes a change in a substance's **chemical properties**. It can also change its **physical properties**. In some reactions, **physical changes** are obvious. In others they are more difficult to notice. Here are some ways to spot chemical reactions.

Bubbling and deposits

Some chemical reactions produce **gases**. When one or both **reactants** is a **liquid**, we can see the gas as bubbles. For example, if we put a piece of chalk in a cup of vinegar, it fizzes. This is because carbon dioxide gas is produced. The **atoms** or **molecules** in a gas are spaced further apart than in a liquid, so they take up a greater **volume**. The gas pushes the liquid out of the way.

Solids can also appear in reactions between some reactants. They look like little crystals or lumps. These solids are called **deposits**.

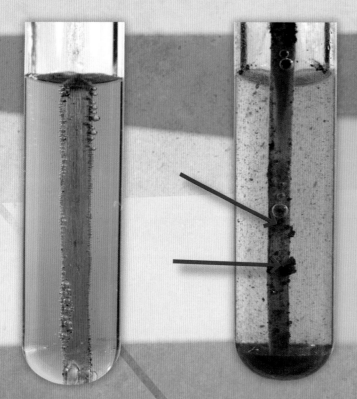

During the reaction between magnesium and copper sulfate mixed with water, copper deposits (see the arrows) form on the magnesium.

Temperature change

All chemical reactions need energy. The energy breaks **bonds** between some atoms and helps new bonds form. Sometimes it takes less energy to make the new bonds than to break the old ones. The extra energy is released, often in the form of heat.

Sometimes it takes more energy to make new bonds than to break the old ones. These reactions take energy from the surrounding area. This makes the surroundings feel colder. If you mix together lemon juice and baking soda in a jar, the jar feels cold. The reaction takes heat energy from your fingers.

Plaster in casts **reacts** with water to set hard. Casts hold broken bones together in the right position so they can mend.

Did you know?
Plaster cast reaction

Have you ever had a plaster cast? Casts are made of cloth coated in plaster of Paris. When the cloth is dipped in cold water, it reacts to form a hard, strong solid. This reaction releases energy as heat. The wet cast starts to feel warm as it sets hard.

Light and color

We can tell some reactions are happening because energy is given off in the form of light. For example, in a lightstick or glowstick there are two substances that react together to produce light. A lightstick only works when you snap it. This is because snapping breaks a brittle plastic tube inside. This allows one reactant to mix with the other.

Many reactions cause a color change because the **product** is a different color than the reactants. In the photograph on page 10, the blue color disappears during the reaction because the product is colorless.

The colored light in fireflies comes from chemical reactions in their bodies.

Did you know?
Light messages

Fireflies are insects that create messages from light to show other fireflies where they are and that they are ready to meet up. The light comes from chemical reactions in their bodies. Fireflies produce new reactants all the time. They can control the reactants and make them glow only at certain times.

Demonstration
Bottle power

You can demonstrate the chemical changes that happen when gas is formed during a chemical reaction. Ask an adult to help you with this experiment.

You will need:
- a small, clean glass bottle with a cork stopper, such as an old vinegar or bath salts bottle
- a tablespoon of vinegar
- a teaspoon of baking powder
- goggles

Procedure:

1 Put the goggles on.

2 Tip the powder into the bottle.

3 Wet the cork with water.

4 Pour the vinegar into the bottle and push the cork in as quickly as possible. Within a minute the cork should pop out!

Explanation

You should see rapid fizzing and bubbling in the mixture as vinegar reacts with baking powder. The reaction produces carbon dioxide gas. The bubbly mixture will rise, filling the bottle. The volume of gas produced soon becomes greater than the space in the bottle. It pushes hard all around the inside of the bottle, but the only part that can move is the cork.

Which Reactions Happen with Oxygen?

Oxygen is a **gas** that makes up about one-fifth of the air surrounding Earth. Some of the most familiar **chemical reactions** are those between oxygen and other substances. These types of reactions are called **oxidation reactions**.

Rusting

If you leave an old bike or other **metal** object outside, it will eventually start to look dull, crumbling, and reddish. The reason is that the surface of the metal has **reacted** with oxygen to form **rust**. Rust is the common name for a **compound** called iron oxide. Rusting is a slow reaction of oxygen with some metals, notably iron and steel, in air and in water. It can happen faster when there is salt in the water or air—for example, by the sea. Iron oxide is weaker than iron. Therefore, the more something rusts, the weaker it gets.

This ship is turning reddish brown. Its steel body reacts with oxygen to form rust.

Experiment

Hot steel wool

Problem: Why does wet steel wool feel hot?

Hypothesis: Metal gets hotter as it rusts because energy is released.

You will need:
- a tall glass jam jar with lid
- dry steel wool
- vinegar
- a thermometer

Procedure:
1 Wrap the steel wool around the end of the thermometer, put it in the jar, and close the lid.
2 Wait five minutes, then record the temperature.
3 Remove the thermometer from the jar. Cover the steel wool with vinegar and soak for two minutes.
4 Pour the vinegar from the jar and squeeze it from the wool. Repeat step 1.
5 Wait five minutes and then record the temperature again.

Results: Did the temperature reading on the thermometer change? If so, did it get higher or lower?

Conclusions: Rusting is a chemical reaction that produces heat. Steel wool starts to rust when it gets wet. The vinegar makes the reaction happen quicker because it removes a coating on the steel that normally protects it from rusting.

Burning

Burning is probably the most common oxidation reaction. Materials only burn when their **atoms** or **molecules** have enough energy to form new **bonds** with oxygen. If they do not have enough energy, they will not burn. For example, candles only burn once the wax is heated by lighting the wick. Once the wick is burning, the wax reacts with oxygen in the air to produce heat and light. Some of this heat keeps the oxidation reaction going.

Burning is a very useful reaction. People burn fuels to create heat. They use the heat to warm their homes, make electricity, and power cars.

Wood is a fuel. When it burns, it creates heat and light.

Did you know?
Animal fuel

All animals, including humans, need to eat food to gain energy. Most food contains a compound called glucose. Our bodies are made up of tiny building blocks called cells. Inside the cells, glucose reacts with oxygen. This reaction is called respiration. It releases energy for growing, living, and moving.

Burning fuel in the engines of this jet can push it forward over six times faster than the fastest Formula One racing car!

Explosive power

When some materials burn, they create enormous amounts of heat and gas very quickly. The materials are called explosives, and the reactions are called explosions. The **volume** of gas suddenly produced pushes very hard against things around it.

Black powder is the oldest known explosive. It was probably first used by Chinese armies around 1,200 years ago. The force of some explosives, such as dynamite, is so great that it can blow things apart. These explosives are used to knock down buildings. Less violent explosions can be used to make things move fast, including rockets and aircraft. In most jet engines on aircraft, a fan blows air and fuel fast past a flame. The fuel burns, creating hot gases that push out of the back of the engine. This pushes against the air, making the aircraft fly forward.

CASE STUDY:

Firework colors

The colored stars you see during a fireworks display are caused by oxidation reactions. During these reactions, different **elements** and compounds burn with different colors. For example, compounds containing copper burn with a blue flame. Compounds that produce colorful lights in this way are called color producers.

At a fireworks factory, fireworks are made by packing different compounds into cardboard and plastic tubes. These include color producers, fuel, and special chemicals that react to produce oxygen. People control the timing of when different stars burst by wrapping color producers in other materials. These have to burn away before the star can appear.

In order to get fireworks into the air, people set fire to small amounts of black powder in the ends of the fireworks. Sometimes they put the fireworks into mortars, which are special guns that fire them into the air.

The different colors of firework are produced by different substances burning.

The Bingham Canyon copper mine in Utah is the largest copper ore mine in the world. It is also the largest man-made hole on the planet!

Ores

Metals are very important materials. We use them to make anything from jewelry and cutlery to large bridges and ships. People mine metals from Earth as **ores**. These are rocks containing large amounts of metals. A few **unreactive** metals, including gold, are usually found as pure metal. However, metals such as iron, copper, and aluminum are found in compounds with other elements. Many of these compounds are metal oxides. This means that metal and oxygen atoms are bonded together.

Chemical reactions can release pure metals from ores. For example, magnetite is a type of iron oxide ore. It is crushed and then heated in a very hot furnace with coke (a material with lots of carbon in it). The carbon in coke bonds with oxygen from the magnetite to form carbon dioxide gas and molten (melted) iron. The **liquid** iron runs out of the furnace. The iron becomes **solid** as it cools.

When Do Reactions Happen More Quickly?

Chemical reactions happen at different speeds. For example, **rusting** is a slow reaction. We can usually speed up reactions by making **reactants** crash into each other faster and more often. There are different ways to make this happen.

Temperature

Many reactions speed up in high temperatures. For example, an egg cooks more quickly in a hot pan than in a warm one. Heat gives **atoms** in any material more energy to move around and form **compounds**.

By striking the tip of a match, the match gets the heat it needs to start burning. The match tip contains glass powder mixed with sulfur. The matchbox has a strip made from glass powder and phosphorus. When you strike the match on the strip, the glass on the match and strip rub together. This creates heat. The heat makes the phosphorus burn. Then, the sulfur catches fire—and then the matchstick.

Strike a match to see a series of **oxidation reactions**!

Light

Some chemical reactions need energy from light to make them happen. For example, newspaper left in strong sunlight for a few days starts to turn yellow. This is because light makes chemicals in the paper **react**. They create compounds with different colors. Newspaper kept in a darker place will turn yellow much more slowly.

Did you know?
Light reaction

Photosynthesis is a chemical reaction that happens in the leaves of green plants. A plant takes carbon dioxide from the air through its leaves and water from the ground through its roots. Sunlight provides the energy needed to make these reactants combine. The **products** of this reaction are glucose and oxygen. Glucose is an important food for plants. This is why green plants grow fast in strong sunlight. They get sickly, weak, and thin if they are grown in poor light.

Trees hold their leaves high up on branches so they get plenty of sunlight. This makes photosynthesis faster. Photosynthesis is a chemical reaction.

Concentration

When you add salt to water, the **chemical properties** of the salt and water do not change. This is a **solution**—a mixture of different atoms or **molecules** that have not reacted together. **Concentration** is a measure of how many atoms or molecules of a substance take up a particular space in a solution. The more salt you mix into a glass of water, the greater the concentration.

Reactions happen more quickly in a more concentrated solution. For example, milk reacts with lemon juice to form curds (**solid** chunks). Curds will form more slowly if you use a mixture of half water and half lemon juice.

All around reactions

The only part of a substance that can react is its surface. The atoms at the surface can combine with other atoms, but the ones inside cannot. For example, coal dust burns more quickly than the same amount of coal in a lump.

Fewer surfaces of wooden bricks are exposed when they are stacked up than when they are spread out. Reactions happen more quickly when the reactants have a larger surface area.

Experiment
Size matters

Problem: A "bath bomb" releases bath salts and scents as it dissolves and spins in bathwater. How can you make a bath bomb fizz faster?

Hypothesis: Small pieces of reactant will react faster than large ones.

You will need:
- three glasses
- three bath bombs
- a teaspoon
- a measuring cup
- a stopwatch, paper, and pencil

Procedure:

1 Put a whole bath bomb into one glass. Break up another into six pieces and put these into the second glass. With the teaspoon, grind the last bath bomb into powder in the third glass.
2 Measure 10 fluid ounces (300 milliliters) of water and pour into the first glass. Time how long it takes for the tablet to stop fizzing.
3 Repeat step 2 for the second and third glasses.

Observations: Each reaction takes a different amount of time. Which reaction was fastest?

Conclusion: You changed the surface area of the bath bomb in two of the glasses. The tablet in the third glass has the largest surface area. Do your observations agree with your hypothesis?

Helping hands

Substances called **catalysts** can help reactions happen faster. Catalysts lower the amount of energy needed to break and make **bonds**.

Yeast is used to make bread rise. It is made up of tiny living things that produce catalysts. These catalysts make sugar in bread dough react quickly with oxygen. The product of this reaction is carbon dioxide. Bubbles of carbon dioxide trapped in bread dough make it rise (grow bigger) before it is baked. Different catalysts are used in making margarine or different types of gasoline.

People use catalysts in yeast to help bread rise.

Did you know?
Catalytic cleaners

Car engines produce exhaust **gases** when they burn fuel. Some of the gases can make the air dirty, or polluted. Catalytic converters are special metal boxes fitted to many car exhaust pipes. Inside are flaps of metal often coated with platinum. This **unreactive** element helps make the gases react with oxygen. They form cleaner gases that do not pollute the air.

How Can We Stop Reactions?

The way to stop reactions is to make sure that the **reactants** do not meet up. There are several ways to do this. One is by lowering the temperature of the reactants. This reduces their energy so they are less likely to collide with one another. Another way is to form a barrier between the reactants so they cannot get to one another.

Stopping fires

People stop fires by spraying water and foam on them. These substances cool the reactants and prevent oxygen from getting to the fuel surface. During forest or grassland fires, firefighters cut down bands of plants called firebreaks. Many fires stop burning at firebreaks as they run out of fuel. However, big fires can continue if firebreaks are too narrow, because hot air blows across the gaps and sets fire to plants on the other side.

This airplane is dumping red powder onto
a bush fire to stop the plants from burning.

Did you know?
Underground fires

Fires deep underground are very difficult to put out because they are hard to reach. Firefighters can spray thick foam containing cement, sand, and water into deep-burning coal mines. This flows around the burning coal, cooling it down and stopping oxygen from getting to it.

Stopping food reactions

Fresh food changes in color and flavor the longer it is kept. This happens partly because **oxidation reactions** take place. People often try to slow food oxidation. One method is to keep it cold in refrigerators or freezers. Another method is vacuum packing. This sucks all the oxygen from around the food in the package. We can also add chemicals that slow down reactions in food.

Drying fruit in sunlight preserves the flavor longer than fresh fruit. People often add preservatives called sulfites to dried fruit such as apricots to stop them from changing color.

In this factory, metal gates and railings are galvanized to help stop them from being damaged by rust.

Using reactivity

People can stop or slow some reactions by adding another more **reactive** substance. The idea is that the reaction uses the other reactant instead. For example, some steel objects that are outside all the time do not **rust** because they are **galvanized**. Galvanized steel has a thin layer of zinc coating its surface.

Zinc is slightly more reactive than the iron in steel. This means that oxygen in air reacts with zinc rather than with iron. Instead of iron oxide (rust), the **compound** formed on the surface is zinc oxide. Iron oxide would crumble away, exposing the steel underneath. Zinc oxide is stronger. It forms a protective layer that keeps oxygen from reaching the steel underneath. People stop the underwater parts of steel ships or ocean pipelines from rusting by attaching lumps of zinc or other **metals** more reactive than iron.

COMPARING REACTIVITY

Reactivity series

Different **elements** have different **reactivities**. For example, potassium is very reactive and **reacts** violently with water and oxygen. Gold is very **unreactive** and will not react with water, even if it is heated strongly. A reactivity series is a list of elements with the most reactive at the top and the least reactive at the bottom.

The reactivity series opposite is just of **metal** elements. Which metals do you think would be best for **galvanizing** iron? Which do you think would burn at lower temperatures?

Potassium (K)

Sodium (Na)

Lithium (Li)

Calcium (Ca)

Magnesium (Mg)

Aluminum (Al)

Zinc (Zn)

Iron (Fe)

Tin (Sn)

Lead (Pb)

Copper (Cu)

Mercury (Hg)

Silver (Ag)

Gold (Au)

This table shows the reactivity series of metal elements.

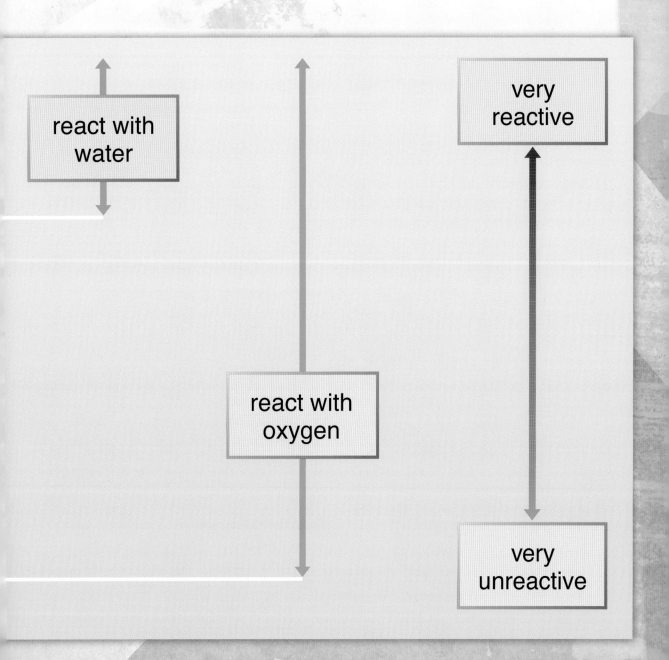

react with water

react with oxygen

very reactive

very unreactive

Glossary

atom one of the tiny particles of which matter is made

bond force caused by electrons pulling atoms or molecules together

catalyst substance that increases the rate of reaction without changing itself

chemical property describes how a substance behaves when combined with other substances

chemical reaction when substances combine to form new substances

chemical symbol letter or letters, often with numbers, used to represent an element or compound

compound substance formed from two or more substances that has different chemical properties than either

concentration measure of mass or volume of a substance in a given volume of solution

deposit solid product from a liquid reactant

electron tiny part of an atom moving around the nucleus

element substance containing one type of atom

galvanize coat in zinc to prevent rusting

gas state of matter in which atoms or molecules are furthest apart

irreversible change that cannot go backward

liquid state of matter in which atoms or molecules are weakly held together with a definite volume but variable shape

magnetism force that causes some metals to move together or apart

mass amount or weight of matter

matter anything with weight that takes up space

metal element, such as iron

molecule two or more atoms joined together

nucleus central part of an atom

ore mineral that contains metal

oxidation reaction chemical reaction such as rusting or burning in which an atom reacts with oxygen

particle very small piece of material

periodic table chart showing all elements arranged by their chemical properties

physical change when measurable or observable physical properties change

physical property characteristic of a substance, such as its state or hardness

product substance produced in a reaction

react undergo a chemical reaction

reactant substance that reacts

reactivity how easily a substance reacts

reversible change that can go backward or forward

rust reddish, crumbly powder formed when iron reacts with oxygen

solid state of matter in which atoms or molecules are packed tightly together in a definite shape

solution when one substance mixes completely with another

unreactive does not easily react

vibrate shake around on the spot

volume space that something takes up

Further Resources

Books

Baldwin, Carol. *Chemical Reactions* (Freestyle *Material Matters* series). Chicago: Raintree, 2006.

Oxlade, Chris. *Elements and Compounds* (*Chemicals in Action* series). Chicago: Heinemann Library, 2002.

Thomas, Isabel. *Fireworks!: Chemical Reactions* (*Physical Science* series). Chicago: Raintree, 2007.

Websites

Lots of different animals use chemical reactions to make light. If you want to know more, visit:
http://www.sdnhm.org/kids/lightsalive/biolum1.html

Index